Albert Frederick Calvert

The Aborigines of Western Australia

Albert Frederick Calvert

The Aborigines of Western Australia

ISBN/EAN: 9783337312602

Printed in Europe, USA, Canada, Australia, Japan

Cover: Foto ©ninafisch / pixelio.de

More available books at **www.hansebooks.com**

THE ABORIGINES

OF

WESTERN

AUSTRALIA.

BY

ALBERT F. CALVERT,

M.E., F.R.S.A., F.R.G.S.A., &C.,

MEMB. BRIT. ASSOC.

*Author of " Hints on Gold Prospecting," " Pearls : Their Origin
and Formation," " The Forest Resources of Western
Australia," " Explorations in North-West
Australia," " The Mineral Resources
of Western Australia," &c., &c.*

𝔏𝔬𝔫𝔡𝔬𝔫:

W. MILLIGAN & CO.,

3a, CAMDEN ROAD, N.W.

1892.

THE ABORIGINES

OF

WESTERN AUSTRALIA.

THE ABORIGINES

OF

WESTERN AUSTRALIA.

R EGARDING the aborigines of Western Australia,
the material for even a short sketch is scanty,
any treatise on the colony, however, would be incom-
plete without some reference to the people who, tor
countless centuries, have roamed over this immense
section of the great island-continent; and in advance
of the general history which I contemplate producing, I
am induced to publish in pamphlet form the following
brief remarks.

There exists a theory that all savages are the de-
graded descendants of civilized ancestors. If this be
true, I think the Australian blackboy's period of
enlightenment must have existed very far back in the dim
twilight of ancient history. Theories however are apt
to out-run facts, so I will not venture to discuss this
question, contenting myself with the observation that
through unnumbered ages there have been wanderers of

the desert side by side with dwellers in cities ; and our black Australian brother seems to have descended from the former class. I am likewise led to remark in passing, that our first parents before the fall did not live in a state of civilization, but of ignorance—an ignorance which was undoubtedly bliss, forever to be dispelled by the knowledge of good and evil. It was after the fall when they had to work and became ashamed of their nude conditions, that they bethought them of the most primitive modes of dress. Thus did civilization and sin enter the world hand-in-hand, soon after the creation.

Among the rudest tribes of men, inhabitants of the wild forests and deserts, dependant for their food and clothing on the accidental produce of the earth or spoils of the chase a form of skull is prevalent, which is termed *prognathous*, indicating an extension forward of the jaws. The facial angle peculiar to this formation is low, and is strongly developed among the Pelagian Negroes of the Eastern Ocean, as well as among the Alfurian or Australian races. They probably spring from a common source ; and the Rev. William Ridley draws attention to the interesting fact that the blacks themselves always have an idea that their ancestors came from the north. Then the current of migration has been ever towards the south and west, and the natives of the north-eastern corner call it " Kai Dowdai " or Little Country. This seems strange when New Guinea is known to them as " Muggi Dowdai " or Great Country. The anomaly is accounted for by their ignorance of the extent of country they inhabit; and to those living near Cape York, and passing to and fro across the strait dividing New Holland from New Guinea, the low narrow promontory would seem insignificant compared with the great mountain ranges of the latter. Then again there is a tradition among some tribes that their first parents landed on the north-west corner from Java. This, however, is but conjecture at best. Their source in short is a mystery buried in the impenetrable mists of an unwritten past.

Although marked differences exist between the various Australian languages, and likewise considerable differences in frame and physiognomy between the various tribes; still the fundamental unity of the population from Swan River to Botany Bay, and from the Gulf of Carpentarie to Bass's Straits is a fact generally admitted. They have no written language, and our alphabet is scarcely adequate to expreesing some of the sounds.

The following are a few of the important dialects spoken :—

Kamilaroi, from the Castlereigh to the Darling, and on the Namai.

Wailwun, on the Barwan, below the junction with the Namai.

Kogai, westward of the Balonne, on the Maranoa and the Cogoon.

Rukumbul, around Calandoon in Queensland ; also on the Weir and Macintyre.

Dippil, about Durundurun on the the north side of Moreton Bay, and thence towards Wide Bay and the Burnett district in Queensland.

Turrabul, on the Brisbane River.

Turruwal, once spoken by the tribe of Port Jackson, now extinct.

Wodi-Wodi, in Illawarra, from Wollongong to the Shoalhaven.

Waradgeri, on the Murrumbidgee and Lauchlan.

Within the boundaries of Western Australia there are numerous dialects spoken. I will only trouble my readers with one illustration. From King George's Sound to Champion Bay a Baby is known as *Good-ja* or *Nuba;* in the New Morcian District, about 80 miles North from Perth, the word is *Chiengallan;* in the Eastern district it would be called *Coo-long*, and in the neighbourhood of Albany, *Culong*. Again at Banbury, Busselton, and along the coast, the infant becomes *Duaing;* at Blackwood, *Noba;* at Champion Bay Victoria district, *Nurellee;* while at Nickol Bay and in the Roeburn district it rejoices in the cheerful name of *Yandeeyarrah.*

A language with such wide discrepancies, no alphabet, and no grammar, presents considerable difficulty to the student.

In Captain William Dampier's book, published in
St. Paul's Churchyard, London, in 1697, he describes
his visit to the North-western coasts of Australia and
quaintly calls the natives " The poor winking people of
New Holland." The circumnavigator bluntly informs
us that they are " the miserablest people in the world,"
and that the *Hodmadods* (Hottentots, I suppose) though
nasty, are gentlemen in comparison ; for the latter have
houses, skin garments, sheep, poultry and fruits of the
earth ; while the former differ but little from brutes.
Then he tells us they are " tall, straight-bodied, and
thin, with small, long limbs; also great heads, round
foreheads, and great brows." Evidently he was much
impressed with their optical eccentricities, for he continues :—" Their eyelids are always half closed to keep
the flies out of their eyes, they being so troublesome
here that no fanning will keep them from coming to
one's face ; and without the assistance of both hands to
keep them off, they will creep into one's nostrils, and
mouth too if the lips are not shut very close. So that
from their infancy being thus annoyed with these insects,
they do never open their eyes as other people; and
therefore they cannot see far, unless they hold up their
heads as if they were looking at somewhat over them."
The outspoken narrator returning to their appearance
declares " They have great bottle-noses, pretty full lips,
and wide mouths. The two front teeth is wanting in all
of them, men and women, old and young ; whether they

draw them out, I know not. Neither have they any beards. They are long-visaged, and of a very unpleasing aspect, having no one graceful feature in their faces. Their hair is short, black and curled like that of the negroes, and not long and lank like the common Indians. The colour of their skins is coal black, like that of the negroes of Guinea.

The poor creatures appear in every way to have excited the pitying contempt of Dampier, inasmuch they had no houses, " the earth being their bed and the Heaven their canopy "; no food except a small sort of fish which they got by making " *wares* of stone across little coves or branches of the sea." These they eked out with cockles, mussels, and periwinkles. Then strange to say they broiled these on the coals, the only respectable sort of thing he noticed about them ; though as to how they got their fire, he confesses his ignorance. Anything in the shape of work they declined to entertain, and when the crafty old mariner gave to one an old pair of breeches, to another a ragged shirt, and to a third a jacket " that was scarce worth owning " expecting the savages in return to " work heartily " at filling the ship's water barrels he was disappointed. As he might have supposed they stood " grinning at him and at one another like so many monkeys."

Such an account as the famous voyager gave in England of his visit to Western Australia in January, 1688, was not calculated to encourage emigration ; nor indeed was the record of his later experiences on the same coast eleven years later.

Now Captain Dampier is looked upon as one of the most intelligent and trustworthy of the English navigators; and I have thus fully quoted his words because his personal descriptions are quaint and forcible. When, however, he states solemnly and pityingly that " The earth affords the natives no food at all"; and that " There is neither herb, root, pulse, nor any sort of grain, nor any sort of bird or beast that they can catch or kill, having no instruments wherewithal to do so." It only proves how erroneous are apt to be superficial or cursory impressions. It may be noted, however, that Dampier's indictment is chiefly directed against the country itself, the natives being treated with a sort of amused commiseration.

Throughout Australia, as in America and elsewhere, the extinction of the aborigines was one of the natural results of colonization. Even where the most humane measures are adopted by some inscrutable power the savage race dies out. The surrounding conditions of life, mental and physical, are entirely changed, and those who collect around townships and stations slowly, but surely follow the fate of others who are killed in conflicts with the settlers.

Upon the white man, alas, most of the responsibility rests. His vicious habits are too faithfully copied by the sons and daughters of the desert, drunkenness and the diseases which follow in its train being a potent factor in thinning the aboriginal ranks.

It is their misfortune to have stood in the way of colonization, and it is scarcely to be wondered at if they have endeavoured to avenge occupation, invasion and robbery of their hunting grounds by deeds of bloody atrocity. It must not be forgotten that the colonists were the aggressors, and that they were often times guilty of crimes against the natives of even more ferocious cruelty. It is indeed a humiliating reflection, that British colonization has done much to destroy, and British Christianity, but little to save, the aborigines. Their degrading customs and brutal crimes have been put forward as a justification for their speedy extinction; while their nobler qualities as true friends and faithful servants have been forgotten. If degradation alone be held to justify extinction, how many subjects of Her Majesty might well be wiped off the face of the earth within a four-mile radius of the British Museum. Civilized human nature is a strange and fantastic compound, whether it owes allegiance to the Union Jack, the Stars and Stripes, the Tricolor, or any flag that flies; is it then to be marvelled at, that we find among these untaught blacks a wild conglomeration of wisdom and folly, nobility and depravity, honour and treachery?

Many of our habits, doubtless, they refuse to imitate. They will cook their food on the embers, but object to boiling or stewing; most kinds of work they rather object to, but smoking and drinking are readily acquired.

Praiseworthy efforts have been made by both Protestant and Catholic Missionaries among the natives of Western Australia, the most successful of which would appear to be that started by Bishop Salvado. Sir F. Napier Broome, G.C.M.G., thus describes the Monastic Institution at New Norcia, — conducted by Spanish Monks,—before the Royal Colonial Institute, a few years ago.

"Australian natives not only sing in church or study in school, but are engaged side by side with the monks in agriculture and various industries; besides playing the violin and other instruments in the Mission Band, and cricket in the Mission Eleven, which visits Perth for an occasional match, and is generally victorious. The New Norcia Mission merits much more notice than time allows me to give it. Its philanthropic and practical work among the aborigines of the colony has now been carried on for more than a generation. Year by year, with infinite pains, labour and expense, it turns a number of the natives into Christian and civilized beings. *The first principle of the work at New Norcia is that it shall go beyond schooling and religious teaching.* I have known a full-blooded low-type savage go forth from this noble mission into civilized life, *not only a good Christian but an expert telegraphist.*"

Lady Barker also writes of this noble monastery of Spanish Benedictines :—" Just below us lay a wide fertile valley, with a large and prosperous village or indeed, town, mapped out by excellent roads and streets, with neat little houses on each side. In the centre stands a good sized chapel, with good schools near it ; and the large monastery on the opposite side of the road seemed to have a splendid garden at the back, stretching down to the river-side." Then she goes on to describe : " A regular stringed band, some eighteen or twenty strong, of native boys ; one playing a big double bass, others violins, a cello, and so forth. Such nice little fellows, black as jet, but intelligent, well-looking, and well-mannered." And adds : " It is impossible to imagine anything more devoted and beautiful than the life their good fathers lead ; and more encouraging than the results of their mission work of about thirty-five years."

The success of these practical earnest and well-directed efforts proves that the Western Australian native is not the intractable human brute which Captain Dampier supposed.

Passing over a period of a century and a half, during which time many other navigators were more or less disappointed if not disgusted by "the poor winking people of New Holland," I notice, that in Juue, 1829, a party of officers and men, under Lieutenant Preston, R.N., landed from H.M.S. *Challenger* at Browne

Mount, Cockburn Sound, for the purpose of exploring the Canning River and intervening country. They were surprised at the absence of natives on this occasion. "But," writes the explorer, "there can be little doubt we passed close to some of them as *we saw several of their wigwams*, and many traces of themselves. It is more than probable they did not like our appearance and avoided us; and from the nature of the country and *their superior power of vision*, they have easy means of concealment." It will be remembered that Dampier imagined that they always slept in the open air, and were almost blind.

Then in September of the same year Lieutenant Preston describes his meeting with the natives, having landed for exploring purposes from H.M.S. *Sulphur* He found them most friendly and intelligent. He gave them a swan, some rings, knives, beads, &c., and received in exchange, spears and a stone hatchet. The shooting of a kangaroo rat astonished them mightily, and they scattered in all directions at the report of the gun. In November, accompanied by Mr. Collie, we examined Geographe Bay, and came across thirty-five natives near Port Vasse. They were most amicable; but shewed considerable shrewdness in bartering, parting with knives, hatchets, and spears only after considerable argument.

Ensign Dale in August, 1831, directed an expedition to the Eastward of the Darling Mountains. He leaves

Perth, we read, on the last day of July, and proceeds to Thompson and Trimmer's on the Swan River; then he picks up Mr. Brockman—his party consisting of a soldier, a store-keeper, and the last-named gentleman. On the 7th of August they discover Mount Mackie, which they named in compliment to the then Chairman of the Court of Quarter Sessions. On the 10th, they arrive at the Dyott Range, called after General Dyott, commanding the 63rd Regiment; the same day finding a litter of native dogs, the mother having left at their approach, and succeeded in bringing two of them alive to Perth. This would have made an interesting little item of news for the "Perth Enquirer;" but the printing-press had not yet arrived from England. Near their bivouac they discover a cavern, the interior being arched and resembling in appearance an ancient ruin. On one side was rudely carved what was evidently intended to represent an image of the sun, it being a circular figure about eighteen inches in diameter, emitting rays from its left side, and having without the circle line meeting each other nearly at right angles. Close to this representation of the sun, were the impression of an arm and several hands. This spot they consider to have been a native place of worship. Again in the same year, we have the record of an excursion in a whale-bout from Rainé. Point to Point d'Estrecasteaux. This explorer, whose name is not mentioned formed very favourable impressions of the natives, who were highly delighted at the catching of snappers with fish-hooks. The narrator goes on to say "Mitchel saw a man on the beach about a mile distant, and with a glass made him out to be a native. I took my gun and walked towards him. After I had gone about half way, and he saw no other person was following me, he advanced and seemed highly delighted when I made him understand I wished him to go to the boat with me; and he very readily gave me his three spears and throwing stick, (which were certainly better made than any I had seen before), and carried my gun to the boat. He appeared astonished when we made him understand that we came from the sea through the breakers." After dressing him, giving him a stocking full of sugar, a little bread, and as much cloth as he chose to carry away, and giving him to understand that he was to go and bring the whole tribe, he departed, but they did not see him again, nor did he bring his friends.

Mr. J. Bussell appears to have made a journey from the Blackwood to the Vasse, about this period, and traverses a tract of country which seems to have enraptured the explorer, for he bursts into poetry.

" With daisies pied, and voilets blue,
" And ladies' smocks all silver white,"

he exclaimes; and then moderating his transports he explains " Though the flowers were not perhaps precisely the same that characterised an English meadow, they were not the less beautiful in appearance, varied in form, or brilliant in colour; grass was plentiful and cloves with bright scarlet and yellow flower, the daisy buttercup and a purple marygold. Truly a pretty picture !

They then met three natives of smaller stature than was usual, and wearing no skins (*sic*). Two were very ugly and brutal looking, but the third sprightly and good humoured in appearance, accompanied with that "revolting laugh so general with these savages." They apparently made themselves very agreeable, and this leads Mr. Bussell to remark that the British population about to flow westward towards the Vasse, may expect a friendly reception from the blacks.

From the foregoing extracts, which I have selected from the original journals in the British Museum, it will be allowed that the natives of West Australia seem to have possessed an average degree of intelligence, and could not be said to belong to the very lowest rank of human beings. In their natural state they cultivate only the qualifications of hunters, and while able to endure privations and fatigue, they are quite unfitted for continuous bodily labour like the whites. In this connection it is laid down by Bishop Salvado, whose authority is unimpeachable, that to condemn a native to hard labour is equivalent to condemning him to death ; and he found it necessary to divide the day's employment, giving three hours to mental, and three hours to bodily labour, the rest of the time being devoted to such relaxation as gymnastics, games, music, and dancing. Their diseases are not amenable to the ordinary course of medical treatment, and native remedies are frequently more efficacious. They pine at times after their forest life, and this home-sickness is best allayed by allowing them an occasional hunting expedition.

Father Garrido asserts that they make good stock-men, teamsters and shepherds, and considers that an agricultural life is the easiest path towards civilization.

Regarding the girls, Mrs. Camfield, superintendent of the school at Annesfield, Albany, reports that they have a great fondness for music. One young woman, who was sent to Sydney, played the harmonium in St. Phillip's Church, and gained her living by teaching. They are likewise taught to wash, cook, and sew,— some marrying civilized natives, and becoming excellent housewives. In the north it may be mentioned that the men supply labour on the settlements and pearl fisheries, and are thus gradually progressing towards civilization. It is therefore by no means apparent that the aboriginal natives must of necessity die out; and this assumption, so placidly accepted by many, is probably due to the havoc wrought among them by that terrible concomitant of civilization—strong drink.

It is often erroneously believed that man in a savage state is endowed with absolute freedom of action; whereas in reality he is subject to a complex system of laws, which not only enslave thought, but allow no scope for intellectual or moral development. These traditional regulations and superstitions keep the Western Australian natives in a condition of barbarism, and cause them to violate many of the most sacred usages of life. For example the female sex are condemned to a degradation which is hopeless, simply because they are defenceless; and this not the result of momentary caprice, but enforced by unwritten traditional laws, which are as binding as those of the Bible or the Koran.

And again, the same or similar traditions have taught the children of the bush how to provide for their natural wants, and well-armed intelligent white men will die of hunger in the desert, where the native will find a sufficiency of food.

One of the most interesting of their laws is that of marriage, which is founded on the fact that they are divided into certain great families, all the members of which bear the family name as a second one in addition to their own. According to Sir George Grey the principal families are the following :—Ballaroke, Idondarup, Ngatak, Nagarnook, Nogonyuk, Mongalung, and Narrangur. Then in different districts the members of these families give a local name to the one to which they belong, which is understood in that district to indicate some particular branch of the principal family.

The most common local names are :—Didaroke, Gwer-
rinjoke, Maleoke, Waddaroke, Djekoke, Kotejumeno,
Namyungo, and Yungaree.

Strange to say these family names are common over
the whole continent. They are perpetuated and spread
throughout the country by two remarkable laws :—

1st. That children of either sex always take their
mother's family name.

2nd. That a man cannot marry a woman of his own
family name.

These singular laws exist among the North American
Indians, and a well-known writer reminds me that a
similar law of consanquinity was probably inferred in
Abraham's reply to Abimeleck (Genesis, Chap. XX.,
Verse 12). "And yet indeed she is my sister ; she is
the daughter of my father, but not the daughter of my
mother, and she became my wife." Each family again
has its *Kobong* or crest. It takes some animal or vega-
table for its sign, and in recognition of this the native
will never kill an animal of the species to which his
Kobong belongs, should he find it asleep ; while his
family vegetable can only be gathered under certain
conditions and at special seasons of the year. The
North American Indians have a similar custom ; thus
we find the Iroquois nation have the turtle, and the
Hurous the bear, as their sign.

Now among civilized nations heraldic bearings are
extensively used, only however by the upper classes.

Strange indeed to reflect that the poor blackboy proudly owns the cognizance of his ancestors in shape perchance of Squirrel, Bandicoot, Iguana, or Kangaroo; while the white settler's knowledge of heraldry is probably limited to a hazy idea that the Lion and the Unicorn are somehow connected with Her Majesty the Queen.

Another very curious law is that which obliges families connected by blood, upon the female side, to unite for the common purpose of defence and avenging crimes. The family name as I have said is that of the mother; and as the father may probably have several wives all of different families, so his children are liable to be divided against each other by deadly feunds. This law would itself prove a hindrance to any people emerging from a savage state. Thus it will be seen that the ties of blood-relationship are as nothing compared with the bond of family; and one of the effects of a father bearing a different name from his children, is that a district of country seldom remains for two generations successively in the same family.

It is not easy to pursue an enquiry into matters of this kind, because another aboriginal law forbids them ever to mention the name of a deceased person, male or female.

Although the natives do not cultivate the soil subsisting entirely by hunting, fishing, wild roots and fruits, it must not therefore be supposed that they have no idea of property in land. Every tribe has its own district, and any intrusion for hunting or other purpose by another tribe would be resisted by force of Arms. Then particular sections of these tribal districts are recognized as the property of individual members, as also the wild animals found upon it ; and each landholder is naturally very jealous of his rights, and pugnacious in upholding them. Trespass for hunting purposes is punished with death if the trespasser be caught in the act ; if he is tracked by footmarks and so discovered he is killed if in a defenceless state, but if attended by his friends he gets off with a spear-thrust through his thigh. The presence of friends even among more enlightened nations has a to mitigate the rigours of the Law.

Death from natural causes is a fallacy in the eyes of the West Australian ; murderers and sorcerers, who cause disease, alone preventing them from living for ever. Someone is therefore always to blame ; and it keeps them pretty busy seeking out the sorcerers and murderers in order to avenge the deaths of their friends. Another principle involved is that if the guilty persons be not found, all his relatives are implicated ; so that the avenging party are nearly sure to have satisfaction out of some one. Again, if there be any hesitation on the part of a native to perform this holiest office of revenge, the females loudly remind him of his duty. His wives will have nothing to say to him, the old women will scold him, and no single girl will even glance at him. The funeral therefore is scarcely over before he seizes his spears, and collecting his friends starts on the warpath. They often find the culprit, and despatch him there and then; but if they fail, their anger becomes so inflamed, that they slay any unfortunate native who falls into their bloodthirsty hands.

Among the West Kimberley natives a curious method is in vogue for discovering the whereabouts of a murderer. The corpse is fixed in the fork of a tree, and in the ground underneath a number of small sticks are stuck pointing north, south, east and west. After the lapse of a few days the friends carefully examine these, and from the droppings of putrid matter which adheres to them, determine in which direction the guilty man is living. I am not aware that this practice is adopted in other parts.

Wife-stealing is punished with the death of the seducer, or one of his relatives.

Minor punishments consist of spear-thrusts through certain portions of the body, such as thigh, calf, arm, etc., a different part being assigned for all ordinary crimes.

Duels are common between individuals who have private quarrels to settle; a certain number of spears being thrown until honour is satisfied. They pay little attention to these wounds, but they soon heal owing to their abstemious habits. Sir George Grey mentions an amusing and striking instance of their apathy, in connection with a fight which took place, in what was then the village of Perth. He says: "A native received a wound in that portion of his frame which is only presented to enemies when in the act of flight; and the spear which was barbed remained sticking in the wound. A gentleman who was watching the fray regarded the man with looks of commiseration, which the native perceiving come up to him, holding the spear (still in the wound) in one hand, and turning round so as to expose the injury he had received, said in the most moving terms, ' Poor fellow, sixpence, give it 'um.' "

Regarding marriage, I should mention that a female child is betrothed in her infancy to some native of another family necessarily many years older than herself. He watches over her jealously as she grows up, and she goes to live with him whenever she feels inclined. If she is pretty she is apt to have a rough time of it; for even if she gives no encouragement whatever to her admirers attempts will be made to carry her off. Encounters resulting she is in great peril; for each combatant orders her to follow him and throws a spear at her if she refuses. The youth of a woman possessing personal attractions is thus full of captures and wanderings, besides scars received at the hands of jealous wives of her abductors. In fact to use the words of the author we have just quoted " Rarely do you see a form of unusual grace and elegance, but it is marked and scarred by the furrows of old wounds; and many a female thus wanders several hundred miles from the home of her infancy.

From the nature of their food, a child must have strong teeth ; hence the mothers suckle them for two or three years, and their families do not average more than four or five in number. Polygamy is general, and women are so highly valued as to be very frequently stolen. This chiefly because they perform all the laborious work, and collect a great portion of the food. Alas ! womens' rights are shamefully neglected and no one takes her part whether innocent or guilty—the general principal being " If I beat your mother, then you beat mine ; if I beat your wife, then you beat mine," and so forth. And yet these poor wild creatures are not devoid of modesty. Their rules as to seclusion correspond remarkably with the law of Moses, as written in Leviticus (Chapters xii. and xv.), while another Mosaic law that of circumcision is observed by the men.

The sympathies of travellers have been much wasted upon the aborigines, on the score of a supposed scarcity of food. As a rule they have an abundance, although they may run a little short in the height of the rainy season or when they are overcome with laziness in very hot weather. The following list of articies forming the food of the West Australian, is from the journal of the last named explorer :—" Six sorts of Kangaroo, twenty-nine sorts of fish, one kind of whale, two species of seal, wild dogs, three kinds of turtle, emus. wild turkeys, two species of oppossum, eleven kinds of frogs, four kinds of fresh water shell-fish, all salt water shell-fish except oysters, four kinds of grubs, eggs of birds and lizards, five animals of the rabbit class, eight sorts of snakes, seven sorts of iguana, nine species of mice and small rats, twenty-nine sorts of roots, seven kinds of fungus, four sorts of gum, two sorts of manna, two species of by-yu, or the nut of the Zamia palm, two species of mesembryanthemum, two kinds of nut, four sorts of fruit, the seeds of several plants." This can scarcely be called a starvation bill of fare.

The equipment of the blackboy consists of his kiley, or boomerang, hatchet, and dow-uk (a short heavy stick), which are stuck in his belt of opossum fur; also his different spears (for war and chase), which with his throwing stick he carries in his hand. In the colder parts he sometimes wears a warm kangaroo-skin cloak, and occasionally a wooden shield curving inwards at the ends. His wife who always follows at a respectful distance is usually in heavy marching order. A long stick is carried in her hand, a bag on her shoulders, in the top of which is fixed any child who cannot walk. The other contents of this useful receptacle are heterogeneous, and complete the stock-in-trade of the family. A flat stone to pound roots with, quartz for making spears and knives, stones for hatchets, prepared cakes of gum for making and mending weapons, Kangaroo-sinews for manufacture of spears and to sew with, the shell of a mussel to cut hair with, different small stone-knives, pipe-clay, red and yellow ochre, are a few of her belongings; and she likewise carries spare skins for cloaks, &c., between the bag and her solely tried back.

They are very skilful hunters, and it is an interesting and beautiful spectacle to watch one of these swarthy savages on the trail, with bright eye and swift, noiseless footsteps. Sometimes they join in company for the chase, which if kangaroo are hunted is *Yowart-a-Kaipoon."* These public pattues are governed by certain rules. The invitation issues from the native owner of the soil, and the first spear which strikes determines whose pro-perty the game is to be, no matter how slight the wound. The animals are surrounded and each man has his position assigned; then the circle gradually closes in on the terrified creatures, but few of whom escape.

The native hunting cries are wild and strange, always commencing with a hard consonant such as " Kau," or " Koo-ee." They are thus audible much further than our " Hullo " or " Ho," which are softer, beginning with an aspirate. They also catch these beasts in nets, pit-falls, and sometimes follow up their tracks until they are so weary as to be approachable. This latter mode requires the very highest class of skill and the greatest endurance ; for which reason only a few of the most re-nowned sportsmen can perform the feat.

Sometimes they roast the Kangaroo whole in a pit which they dig for the purpose ; and occasionally cut it up and broil the portion piecemeal. The blood, the en-trails, and the marrow are considered delicacies, and are reserved for the head men of the tribe. They catch fish in three different ways—spearing them, entrapping them in a weir (referred as a " ware " by Dampier) and netting them. In the first method they shew marvellous skill, whether in rivers or in the sea, and seldom miss their aim. The weirs they construct at low water, showing considerable sagacity in the selection of its locality.

Probably the greatest joy which a native knows is the discovery of a stranded whale upon his property. As a rule he is very greedy in sharing his food ; but such an abundance changes his whole nature, so he lights fires and invites all his friends. Then a disgusting orgie en-sues, for they stay by the carcase long after it is putrid— sometimes for weeks ;—then having made themselves and their children extremely ill, they carry it off in evil-smelling chunks, as presents for their relatives who have missed the treat.

They enjoy eating wild-dog for a change, but puppies are specially prized. They are often saved, however, for other domestic purposes, when one of the mothers of the family suckles them at her own breast. Australia being the land of black swans and other contraries, we need not be surprised to find this reversal of the story of Romulus and Remus. Like London Aldermen the natives are very partial to turtle, and are not surpassed by the New Yorkers in their appreciation of terrapin. The latter they cook whole, shell and all in the ashes; then removing the bottom shell, the upper one serves as a dish. Most delicious of all, however, is accounted the emu, and hence it follows that heavy penalties are pronounced by the law-makers of the nation against any one eating this bird but themselves.

Cockatoos are often killed with the boomerang, and to see this strange weapon swooping wildly among a flock of these birds,—spinning, and whirling and slaying is one of the oddest sights imaginable. One of the dexterous feats which Sir George Grey recounts is the killing of a bird as it flies from the nest. Two men are engaged in it, one of whom, placing himself under the nest, transfixes it with a spear. As a rule the creature is only frightened or very slightly wounded, and is slain by the unerring dow-uk of the other hunter as it quits the tree. In opossum hunting the savage climbs the tree, which he notches into footholds as he proceeds; then either smokes or prods the animal out of his hole, when he seizes it by the tail and dashes it to the ground—always careful, however, to avoid being bitten. Frog-catching, when the swamps are partly dried up, is usually the duty or pastime of the women. It is no easy task, however, for while poking about with their long sticks in the mud, they are almost devoured with flies and mosquitos.

Grubs, which are extremely palatable, are procured

from the grass-tree; and likewise in an excrescence of the wattle-tree. They are eaten either raw or roasted, but are improved by cooking.

To the females is likewise assigned the duty of digging the various roots at which they are very expert; these they sometimes pound and mix with a kind of earth, and sometimes roast plain. They also collect the *by-yu* nut, of which the kernel is a violent cathartic—as Captain Cook's sailors found to their cost. There is a pulp, however, which encases this inner kernel, which after certain preparation, is an agreeable and nutritious article of food. Many other objects of the chase and species of diet are known to the natives to which limited space forbids reference.

In his admirable play of " The Mourning Bride," Congreve declares that

" Music hath charms to soothe the savage breast,
" To shelter rocks, and rend the solid oak."

If the dramatist tells us a little more than the truth in the second line. I think he falls short of the whole truth in the first.

The West Australian warrior, at least, is devoted to music, but it has scarcely a soothing effect when it takes the form of one of his war-songs. He rushes to and fro, brandishing his weapons in a rapidly increasing frenzy. Here is a specimen of what he sings :—

" Yu-do dan-na,
Nan-do dan-na,

My-eree dan-na,
Goor-doo dan-na,
Boon-ga-la dan-na,
Gonogo dan-na,
Dow-al dan-na,
Nar-ra dan-na,"
&c., &c.

Which, being interpreted, means :—
" Spear his forehead,
Spear his breast,
Spear his liver,
Spear his heart,
Spear his loins,
Spear his shoulder,
Spear his thigh,
Spear his ribs,"
&c., &c.

When we consider our very slight knowledge of their language, feelings and passions; it is not surprising that we fail to appreciate the niceties of their music and poetry. Nevertheless it is a fact that an elderly and spiteful female, who posseses musical and poetic gifts, can set a score of warriors thirsting for each others blood.

Mr. Threlkeld, in his Australian Grammar, says :— " There are poets among them who compose songs which are sung and danced to by their own tribe in the first place ; after which other tribes learn the song and dance—which itinerates from tribe to tribe throughout the country—until, from change of dialect, not one of the original words remain."

A new song is highly appreciated, and a native gentleman who has travelled to distant parts, sometimes brings back a few of the latest, with which, no doubt, " he astonishes the natives ! "—certainly they are very savage-sounding and discordant ditties to European ears ; but, on the other hand, our music is most flavorless, insipid and ridiculous to the aboriginal taste. An imitation of one of our songs by a native, for the amusement of his relatives and friends, never fails to produce shrieks of astonishment and laughter. Doubtless the black looks upon us as a very absurd and eccentric race of mortals. I am reminded of Robert Burns' words in his address to the lowest type of insect :—

> " O wad some power the giftie gi 'us,
>   To see oorsel's as ithers see us ;
>   It wad frae mony a blunder free us,
>   And foolish notion."

The only accompaniment to the songs I have observed, is the beating of a board or clapping of hands. Any remarkable circumstance which occurs is likely to be perpetuated by a song. Sir George Grey tells us that when Miago,—the first native who ever quitted Perth, —was taken away in H.M. surveying vessel Beagle in 1838, the following song was composed by a relative and constantly sung by his mother during his absence.

It begins thus :—

" Ship bal win-jal bat-tar dal gool-an-een,
Ship bal win-jal bat-tar dal gool-an-een," &c., &c.

Meaning,

"Whither is the lone ship wandering,
Whither is the lone ship wandering," &c., &c.

Then, on his safe return, the same poet recounted his voyage thus :—

" Kan de maar-o, Kan de maar-a-lo,
Tsail-omar-ra, tsail-o mar-ra-lo," &c., &c.

Meaning,

" Unsteadily shifts the wind oh ! unsteadily shifts shifts the wind oh !
The sails-oh handle, the sails-oh handle ho !"

&c., &c.

It is impossible to describe the strange wild music of these swarthy denizens of the forest ; but the abundant evidence of passion and feeling which it expresses, should forbid too hasty a judgment of a people of whom we really know so little.

Regarding the religion of the aborigines, the evidence is somewhat conflicting. Certain it is that their legends are full of evil spirits and malignant demons which destroy men, women, and children. I think it is very doubtful if they have any knowledge of a beneficent God or righteous Creator. *Mullion* is a wicked being who lives in a high tree and seizes blackfellows to devour a higher abode for he lives in the Milky Way. Then there are some female demons who are much more cruel and implacable; one particularly, who impales the poor black with her spear and carries him off wriggling and writhing to her den, where she roasts and eats him. Then there is a famous creature called the *Bunyip*, a terrific monster (somewhat like our sea-serpent, surely). for it is some fifty feet long, with a snake-like head, and inhabits lagoons, rivers, and swamps. *The Bunnyar* is a kind of Western Australia *Bunyip*, and from the peculiarities of this evil beast, it is probable that the stories of the alligators in the North of Australia and Queensland have penetrated other parts of the country, and formed the basis for this special water demon.

Piame is in some district a word which signifies the father of the black people, and may be taken to indicate a beneficient Diety; and there are periodical celebrations and ceremonies which seem to set forth a conflict between good and evil influences.

Such ceremonies may have come across from Asia in bygone ages, or may be inventions of the Australian soil.

Be that as it may, Christianity is undoubtedly the chief factor towards civilization; and has been by far the most potent agent in raising these wild natives from the dark depths of savagery in which they exist.

The aboriginal funeral ceremonies are somewhat different in various parts of the continent, and vary

tbem ; Wurrawilburu is another evil spirit, who has even
even throughout that portion to which this paper is
devoted. In illustration of this, and because the subject
possess considerable interest, I shall quote three descriptions from the pens of the aforesaid Sir George
Grey, Mr. Bussel, and Mr. Scott Nino.

The first took place at Perth in June, 1839. "There
were but few men present," writes (the then) Captain
Grey, "as they were watching the widows in Perth,
Yeuna and Warrup, were digging the grave, which as
usual extended due east and west. They commenced
by digging with their sticks and hands several holes in
a straight line, and then united them. All the white
sand was thrown carefully into two heaps, and these
heaps were situated one at the head, and the other at
the foot of the hole ; whilst the dirty coloured sand was
thrown into two other heaps, one on each side. The
grave was very narrow, just wide enough to admit the
body. During the process of digging—an insect having
been thrown up—its motions were watched with intense
interest, and as it thought proper to crawl off in the
direction of Guildford, an additional proof was furnished
that the sorcerer resided there. When the grave was
completed, they set fire to some dried leaves and twigs,
and throwing them in, soon had a large blaze. Old
Weeban knelt on the ground at the foot of the grave, his
head bowed to the earth in profound attention. He was
watching to discover in which direction the *boyl-yas* or

sorcerer, when drawn from the earth by the fire, could take flight.

At last he indicated a due east direction with his spear, and a smile of satisfaction irradiated the faces of the young men ; for they know that towards Guildford they must go to avenge the foul witchcraft which had slain their brother-in-law. The next part of the proceedings was to take the body from the females. They raised it in a cloak, his old mother making no objection to its removal ; but passionately kissing the cold rigid lips which she could never press again. The corpse was then lowered into the grave and seated upon a bed of leaves which had been laid there directly the fire was extinguished, the face being turned towards the east. The women grouped together, sobbed forth their mournful songs whilst the men placed small green boughs upon the body, until they had more than half filled up the grave. Then cross pieces of wood were fixed in the opposite sides of the grave, green boughs placed on these, and the earth from the two side heaps thrown in, until the grave was completed; which then, owing to the heaps at the head and foot, presented the appearance of three graves, nearly similar in size and form, lying due east and west.

The men having completed their task, the women came with bundles of blackboy tops which they had gathered and laid these down on the central heap, so as to give it a green and pleasing appearance."

The following is extracted from a letter written by
Mr. Bussel, when resident near the Vasse River,
Western Australia. A native herdsman employed by
Mr. Bussel had been murdered. The master writes.—
The funeral is a wild and fearful ceremony. Before I
had finished in the stock-yard, the dead man was already
removed and on its way to the place of interment, about
a quarter of a mile distant. I was guided to the spot
by the shrill wailing of the females, as they followed
mourning after the two men who bore the body in their
arms. The dirge, as distance blended all the voices,
was very plaintiff; nor did the distance destroy the
harmony. Some of the chants were really beautiful;
but perhaps rather harsh for our ears. They produced
a terrible jarring on my brain and caused tears to flow
even from the eyes of infants, who knew nothing of
the cause of the lament. At length the procession
reached the place, and there was a short silence.
When the body touched the ground a piercing shriek
was given, and as this died away into a chant some of
the elder women lacerated their scalps with sharp bones,
until the blood ran down their faces in streams. The
eldest of the bearers stept forward and proceeded to dig
the grave. 1 offered to dig the grave, but they refused:
the digging stick was the proper tool, and when with
this the earth was loosened, it was thrown out in
showers with the hands, forming in the same line with
the grave two elongated banks.

At length the grave was finished, and they then threw some dry leaves into it and kindled a fire. When this had burnt out, they placed the corpse beside the grave and gashed their thighs, saying at the flowing of the blood:—" I have brought blood ; " and they stamped the foot forcibly on the ground, sprinkling the blood around them. Then wiping their wounds with wisps of leaves, they threw in the dead man. Then a loud scream ensued, and they lowered the body into the grave, resting on the back. They filled up the grave with soft brushwood, and piled logs on this to a considerable height ; after which they construct a hut over the woodstack.

The third description is from the Journal of the Royal Geographical Society. The ceremony took place at King George's Sound, the narrator being Mr. Scott Nind, who says :—

" Their funeral ceremonies are accompanied by loud lamentations. A grave is dug about four feet long, and three feet wide, and perhaps a yard in depth. The earth that is removed is arranged on one side of the grave in the form of a crescent. At the bottom is placed some bark and then small green boughs ; and upon this the body, ornamented and enveloped in its cloak, with the knees bent up to the breast, and the arms crossed. Over the body are heaped more green boughs and bark, and the hole is then filled with earth, Green boughs are placed over the earth, and upon them are deposited the spears, knife, and hammer of the deceased, together with the ornaments that belonged to him ; his throwing-stick on one side, and his Kiley and dowak on the other side of the mound. The mourners then carved circles in the bark of the trees that grow near the grave ; and lastly, making a small fire in front they gather small boughs, and carefully brush away any portion of earth that may adhere to them. Their faces are coloured black or white in blotches across the forehead, round the temple, and down the cheek bones ; and these marks are worn as mourning for a considerable time. They also cut the end of the nose, and scratch it for the purpose of producing tears."

There is thus, it will be seen considerable diversity in the burial rites of the different tribes. One point, however, which they all appear to attend to, is a careful investigation regarding the *boyl-yas* or sorcerer who has caused the death. They are always objects of mysterious dread, having power they believe to transport themselves through the air in invisible form. Sometimes another monster is to blame, called the *wau-gul* ; it resides in fresh water, and usually attacks females who pine away and die under its baleful influence.

It has been said elsewhere that the physical features of Western Australia resemble, in many respects, those of the Holy Land. Both suffer from periodical draughts, and largely depend on wells for water ; then both have fertile and smiling pastures, side by side with barren sandy wastes; both have a warm summer and a pleasant sea breeze near the coast, and both have largely a limestone formation. Still more curious to notice is the similarity of some points between the customs of the aborigines and those of the ancient Jews. The superstitious rites remind us of I Kings, xviii, 28 :— " And they cried aloud, and cut themselves after their manner with knives and lancets, till the blood gushed out upon them." Then again Jer. xlvii, 37, " For every head shall be bald, and every beard clipped ; and upon all the hands there shall be cuttings, &c."—In some parts of Australia, the natives cut off portions of their beards at funerals in addition to the lacerations. Again in Deut. xiv. 1, it is written " Ye shall not cut yourselves, nor make any baldness between your eyes for the dead. " Evidently this was an ancient Jewish custom forbidden by Moses ; and we find that when the native females cut and scratch their faces in mourning for the dead, their favorite place for tearing the skin is *between the eyes* as forbidden." Isaiah, in chapter xlv., verse 4 and 5, reprehends remaining amongst the graves : —" A people which provoke me to anger, &c., which remain among the graves and lodge in the monuments." The native form of taking a oath also is very much akin to that described in Genesis xxiv., 9, " And the servant put his hand under the thigh of Abraham his master, &c." Then the Australian mothers constantly name their children from some circumstance connected with

their birth, or early infancy ; just as in Genesis xxx, 11,
" Leah said, A troop cometh, and she called his name
Gad."

I have already referred to the practice of circumcision,
which is common in many parts from St. Vincent's
Gulf to the Gulf of Carpentaria.

I have alluded to the interesting coincidences, but
make no attempt to draw inferences therefrom. With
but meague data and inadequate knowledge, the subject
is unapproachable. If, however, these primitive people
should have received from the common Creator certain
laws for the guidance of their lives, does it not furnish
food for reflection ? It is scarcely necessary that I
should disclaim any intention of identifying my aboriginal friends with the Lost Tribes !

I have already mentioned the kiley or boomerang as a
native weapon, but this most extraordinary implement
deserves special attention. Its possession alone, I
contend, redeems the Australian savage from his usually
assigned place at the foot of the human ladder. Doubtless other nations—notably the Africans and Indians—
have an instrument of somewhat similar form, but the
main characteristic is wanting, namely, the *return flight*.
Its usual form is a piece of hard wood with the curve of
a parabola, about two feet long, two and a half inches
broad, one third of an inch thick, and rounded at the
extremeties. One side is flat, the other rounded, and it
is brought to a bluntish edge. It is discharged by the

hand at one end, the convex edge being forward, and the flat side upwards. After advancing some distance and ascending slowly in the air with a quick rotatory motion, it begins to retrograde, often falling to the ground behind the thrower. The scientific reason for this is clear. As long as the boomerang feels the forward impetus and catches the air—as it will naturally do—on the flat side, it continues to rise. When, however, the movement of transition ceases, it begins to fall; and its course of falling will be in the line of the least resistance, which is in the direction of the edge that lies obliquely towards the thrower. It will therefore fall back, in the same manner as a kite when the string is suddenly broken, is seen to fall back a short distance. But the kite, having received no rotation to cause it to continue in the same plane of descent, soon falls in a series of fantastic curves to the ground; as also will the boomerang if it loses its rotatory motion.

Now it is evident that this marvellous property of the boomerang (founded, however, on a recognised law of projectiles), must be of great advantage to the natives; for it is largely used for throwing among flocks of fowl in rivers, lakes, and marshes; when after striking (or missing) its object, instead of being probably lost, it returns to the owner. There are several varieties of boomerang, but they all follow this unique law, dependant of course to some extent on the skill of the thrower. Could any device be more strangely ingenious?

Here is a fair sample of native humour, if not common sense. A well-known explorer, some fifty years ago, worn out with fatigue, and weak from privations, flung himself by the fire to rest, having almost reached Perth on his return journey. His wretched and woebegone appearance attracted the attention of the native who accompanied him. He had some knowledge of English, and thus addressed his master : " What for do you who have plenty to eat, and much money, walk so far away in the bush " ?

The explorer tired to death, and rather annoyed at this conundrum, made no answer. The black went on : " You are thin, your shanks are long, your belly is small—you had plenty to eat at home, why did you not stop there ? " It is hard to make these simple folk understand the love of enterprise and adventure, so the traveller had to say

" Oh, you don't understand : you know nothing."

" I know nothing ! " he exclaimed with a laugh, " I know how to keep myself fat ; the young women look at me and say, ' He very nice, he fat.' They look at you and say, ' No good, he too thin legs too long, he walk too far in the bush.' "

It cannot be denied that to all appearance the Englishman had the worst of the argument.

Idiocy is almost unknown among the natives, and I never heard of a native lunatic. Such an afflicted person would probably soon be suspected as a *boyl-ya* or sorcerer, and a few spear-thrusts would put a speedy end to him and his malady.

The hardships of ordinary bush life soon kills off the weaklings, and the surviving savages usually possess constitutions of iron. Child-desertion is the only form of infanticide known. This, however, is not considered a crime, but a necessity; so that if a female is ovre-burdened with young children, she leaves her new-born infant to starve, and troubles herself no further about it. Suicide is unknown, and the natives are rather amused at the idea of anyone being such an arrant fool as to deprive himself of life. Such a height of folly is only attainable by a white man! Extradition exists to a certain extent among these savages; and in cases of murder, adultery, or abduction, if the offending party should happen to take refuge with another tribe, the headmen of his own community decide that he must be punished with death. The tribe or clan harbouring the culprit is then requested to deliver him up to justice. If this request is granted, as is usually the case, the nearest relatives of the injured or murdered person, kill him on the spot. If, however, the sheltering tribe should refuse to give him up, war is proclaimed there and then.

The foregoing hurriedly gathered facts connected with the West Australian natives, to shew that they are men of like passions with ourselves, and not merely on a level with the beasts that perish. The present state of the free coloured population of the United States, proves how high in the social scale a once savage race can rise. Christianity demands that we should do all in our power for the amelioration of these people, whose lands we have taken, giving them in return the somewhat doubtful privilege of being British subjects. This responsibility is forced upon us by our own acts: let us not seek to evade it ; but mindful of the rich lands and mighty country which these wild races have surrendered, manfully do our duty by our dark-skinned fellow-subjects.

There are those who flatter themselves that they belong to a higher order of created beings than the Western Australian aborigines, who have been represented as mere baboons possessing an innate deficiency of intellect, which renders them incapable of instruction or civilization.

It will be well for such persons to reflect that a similar opinion was one timê held by the cultured Romans concerning the aborigines of Great Britain.

Cicero in one of his epistles to Atticus, thus refers to our ancestors :—

" Do not " says he " obtain your stores from Britain, because they are so stupid and utterly incapable of being taught, that they are not fit to form a part of the household of Atticus."

W. MILLIGAN & CO., 3a, CAMDEN ROAD, LONDON, N.W.

www.ingramcontent.com/pod-product-compliance
Lightning Source LLC
Chambersburg PA
CBHW031816090426
42739CB00008B/1303